What's That I Hear?

Activities to Develop
Listening Skills
in Children 3-8

by Sam Ed Brown, Ph.D.
Illustrations by Silas Stamper

**Communication
Skill Builders**

3830 E. Bellevue/P.O. Box 42050
Tucson, Arizona 85733
(602) 323-7500

About the Author

Sam Ed Brown received his undergraduate degree at the University of Chattanooga in Tennessee. He holds a master's degree from the University of Tennessee and a Ph.D. from Florida State University. Dr. Brown is currently a Professor of Early Childhood Education at Texas Woman's University, Denton, and is the author of several books and articles in the educational field.

© 1986 by

Communication
Skill Builders, Inc. ®
3830 E. Bellevue/P.O. Box 42050
Tucson, Arizona 85733
(602) 323-7500

ISBN 0-88450-958-3   Catalog No. 7282

10   9   8   7
Printed in the United States of America

Contents

Listening Skills in Young Children

Children have always used listening as a means of learning from parents and teachers, but the contemporary youngster is actually bombarded with verbal directions and commands. In addition to verbal instruction from teachers, many early childhood classrooms are using television sets and computers for educational purposes. The learning that occurs in a video presentation is more auditory than visual and even computers demand certain auditory skills.

Most children can *hear* when they are born. Research bears out the fact that early in life children develop the ability to *listen* selectively. Since listening is a learned skill, there are many children who do not learn how to do it.

Some teachers may have problems teaching listening skills because not enough emphasis is placed on these skills in colleges and universities. We are led to believe that children with listening problems are children with hearing problems and this certainly is not always the case.

When listening is discussed, it sounds like a fairly simple skill. The child either listens or not. However, there are at least four steps involved in listening:
    1. Recognizing sounds
    2. Giving meaning to sounds
    3. Determining response
    4. Integrating these areas

The first thing a child must do is learn to recognize sounds, which means that the child recognizes a sound as one that has been heard before. For example, the child becomes used to hearing a clock strike. The child learns that the striking clock sounds the same each time.

Giving meaning to sounds from past experiences is a little more complicated because the child must be able to associate a sound with something known or experienced. If you tell children that it is hot outside, they will understand because they have played outside on hot days, observed people in hot weather, and listened to the weather forecast on radio and television. A problem arises when you tell the child that it is 37 degrees Celsius. Not being exposed to metric measure, the child either thinks it is cold outside or doesn't understand what is being talked about.

1

Recognizing a sound and being able to associate it with past experiences is not enough. The child must also know what kind of reaction to the sound is required. Background sounds demand no action. Other sounds such as the ringing of a phone or the honking of a car horn require some form of action.

The final integration of recognizing a sound, associating the sound with past experiences, and determining the action that must be taken is a learned skill in which a child must become proficient.

It is difficult to determine if a child is actually listening. It is possible that a child who seems to be just sitting and shows no response to what is being said may have complete understanding of the communication. Some children are active listeners as long as the conversation is about them or about something in which they have a strong interest. These same children may tune out any other conversations. Children who are more interested in talking than listening rarely hear what is being said because they are too busy thinking about what they are going to say.

Often children who are just starting preschool have already developed methods of listening, depending on their environment. To realize improvements with a child, teachers and caregivers must be aware of how that child listens, which involves knowing the child's areas of weakness and strength.

Most children have already developed *appreciative listening* skills, or *auditory appreciation,* and find pleasure in listening to stories, poems, and music. Some children may not have been exposed to experiences that lead to this type of listening.

To express thoughts spontaneously and freely through words or actions, a child must have developed *creative listening* skills. The child's imagination and emotions are stimulated by listening experiences.

Not all children are exposed to *rhyming* in early childhood. In preschool, kindergarten, or in the early grades, they may need to be taught to recognize and reproduce words that rhyme.

Remembering sequence within words and sentences is *auditory memory.*

Many children are deficient in *purposeful listening,* which means they cannot follow directions or respond appropriately.

An awareness of changes in pitch and loudness is *discriminative listening* or *auditory discrimination.* This area also includes the ability to differentiate sounds in the environment.

Relating sounds to experiences, objects, ideas, known facts, or feelings is *auditory association.*

The ability to perceive and understand what is heard is *auditory perception.*

Critical listening skills allow children to understand, make decisions, and formulate opinions. A child must be able to think through responses to questions, decide the most logical solution to the problem, and present a point of view.

Each of the above skill areas includes even more specific listening skills such as following directions, gleaning information, and solving problems.

LEARNING FROM LISTENING

Vocabulary develops primarily through the child's interaction with parents, day-care workers, and teachers. While some words are learned by watching and listening to television, the activity is usually not in-depth enough to build vocabulary.

The ability to use correct syntax, or to form understandable sentences, comes from the same sources as vocabulary. Talking with peer groups and significant others is also influential.

Every culture has a language element called *prosody.* This involves, among other things, the inflections one uses when talking. Sentences can take on different meanings depending on the inflections used. Only by listening can a child realize the significance of inflections.

Listening also adds to conceptual development. As the adult explains the difference between a house and a mobile home or between a bicycle and a motorcycle, the child's concept must change to accept this difference.

Parents and teachers may assume that a child who has been screened for hearing difficulties and passed knows how to listen, but this is not always the case. Some children, instead of developing listening skills, have learned to tune out what doesn't interest them. For example, children who are constantly criticized at home learn to tune out conversation. Often these children use this same skill to tune out the teacher.

Children are constantly surrounded by sounds. It is vital that they learn to listen selectively, that is, to listen and respond to significant sounds while letting background sounds pass by. This is a learned skill.

AN INTEGRATIVE APPROACH

During recent years, research has been conducted on the functions of the two hemispheres of the brain. Different functions for each hemisphere have been identified.

The left hemisphere is sometimes called the *talking brain* and it is the logical, analytical portion of the brain. This hemisphere specializes in thinking from the part to the whole and plays a large role in problem solving based on facts read and heard.

The right hemisphere is sometimes called the *silent brain* or the *creative brain.* It thinks in pictures and sees the whole instead of the parts. This hemisphere also excels in tactile and visual information.

A bundle of nerves called the *corpus callosum* connects the two hemispheres and allows information to flow between them.

How the two hemispheres cooperate is illustrated in the following example: A child sees or hears the word "cat" for the first time. This information is processed by the left hemisphere and enters the short-term memory bank. Meanwhile, the child sees a picture of a cat and pets a real cat. This visual and tactile information is processed by the right hemisphere and is then shared with the left hemisphere. Such integration of information results in the true concept of "cat" and is much more likely to move from short-term to long-term memory.

Auditory perception and auditory discrimination are both left-hemisphere specializations. Auditory association and rhyming skills are better handled by the right hemisphere. Auditory memory can be achieved only through cooperation of both hemispheres.

It can be readily understood, then, that while we aim to teach or reinforce skills in one particular area, we must at the same time employ other areas in the process. For example, we reinforce auditory perception and attentive listening by reading aloud a story and then asking the children to draw a picture. This requires children to associate the picture created by the right hemisphere. By acting on the concept, the child is integrating information from both hemispheres.

Suggestions for Teaching Listening Skills

1. Make allowances for children's short attention spans.
Children's attention spans are in direct proportion to their interest in the subject matter. Short attention spans can be coped with or increased without undue pressure by adhering to the following guidelines.

    a. Plan brief periods of any one activity, but be prepared to extend that activity if the children show a great amount of interest.

    b. Be flexible. Just because an adult thinks a certain activity is fun and exciting, it does not necessarily follow that children feel the same way. A flexible teacher recognizes when children are not enjoying an activity and is willing to change to something they want to do.

    c. Vary activities, using bright colors and appealing pictures as teaching aids. Children dearly love finger plays and will listen carefully when they are being used. Rely on finger plays for transition times and whenever you want the children to listen.

    d. Don't interpret wiggling, moving, and talking as indicators of lack of interest. Almost all young children have difficulties sitting still for long periods.

    e. Arrange a comfortable environment for the children. Is the room too hot? Too cold? Is it too crowded? Is the room carpeted or are mats available so the children can sit comfortably on the floor?

2. Help children realize that listening is important.
    a. Model good listening habits for the children. Make it a practice to signal the room to silence when something is being announced over the speaker or when someone is speaking to the entire class. In this way, children learn that it takes some effort to become a good listener.

    b. Talk in your normal speaking voice so the children must listen to hear what you are saying. Don't compete with the noise in the room. As the child's preschool or kindergarten teacher, be aware that you are the child's first professional teacher. In this role, you must always be aware of vocabulary and speak in an even and well-controlled voice.

c. If some children are not listening, do not repeat the same instruction over and over.

d. Monitor the time you spend talking. Research will bear out that 65-75 percent of the talking in classrooms is done by an adult.

e. Begin every day with a conversation time in which the children are allowed to talk about anything that interests them. Require the children who are not speaking to give the speaker their attention.

3. Give children time.

Children should not be expected to follow one direction after another, especially if they are not expecting the directions. Prepare children to receive directions and give them time to get ready to listen. First, get their attention, then tell them to put away what they are working with and get ready to listen.

4. Set a good example.

When a young child wants to talk, move down to the child's level, look the child in the face and listen. Respond verbally to the child whether it involves answering a question or giving directions. During a busy day in the classroom, it is often difficult to listen to every child. However, a child who is trying to tell you about an observation believes that this observation is of the utmost importance. Make your best effort to hear and respond to each child.

5. Create a relaxed, happy atmosphere.

In a relaxed atmosphere between adult and child and among the children themselves, children will usually listen. A child who is uneasy, hostile, or afraid will have problems listening.

6. Help the children develop an awareness of sounds they hear every day.

Encourage children to call attention to strange sounds. Have them close their eyes and identify sounds they hear. Some simple listening games are described in activities 1, 7, and 14.

7. Provide opportunities for a wide variety of listening experiences for pleasure, appreciation, and information.

a. Show numerous films and read many stories to encourage listening for information. The importance of reading to children cannot be over-emphasized. Take advantage of every opportunity to read aloud well-written and enjoyable books. Activities 42, 45, and 51 present ways to use stories as listening tools.

b. Music is another area that greatly aids children in developing listening skills. Singing requires that children remember songs and listen for their particular singing parts. More interest in sounds, how to make them, and how to differentiate between them will occur if children make their own instruments for a rhythm band. Directions are given in activities 78 and 81.

c. Tape the children's favorite stories so they can listen to the story as they read the book. Activity 54 shows how this can be structured.

d. Provide comfortable, attractive conversation "pits" and encourage the children to use these places for discussions. Activities 96, 97, and 98 provide topics for discussion as well as the conversation cues at the end of all the activities.

e. Encourage dramatic play where children take parts and have to listen for their cues. See activities 49 and 55.

f. Encourage children to bring in interesting items from home and tell the class about them. Follow this by a question and answer period related to the items. Activities 28 and 29 are based on this idea.

g. If appropriate, discuss listening activities with parents. Reproduce the following two pages for the parents to use with the child in home activities.

A Note to Parents

Most children are born hearing but without skills for listening. These skills begin to develop in the home. The better developed these skills become, the more success your child will have in school. To give your child a good start, constantly take advantage of ways to increase or refine your child's developing skills.

As an adult, you interact with other adults while continuing with whatever task is at hand. With children, it is necessary to model listening skills by stopping what you are doing when the child speaks to you. Bend to the child's level to listen. This conveys to the child that not only is what is being said of value, but careful listening is important.

In your environment, you have become used to hearing many sounds. You react to some and not to others. The young child hears these same sounds but does not understand their sources or how they are made. Share sounds with children in the following ways:

- Call attention to such sounds as the doorbell ringing and explain to the child how the doorbell works.

- Take children on listening walks in the woods or along the street. Listen for unfamiliar sounds. Investigate them and explain how they are made.

- While reading to your child, make your voice sound like the different characters in the story. Later, talk to your child in one of those voices and see if the child can identify it.

Often when young children listen to music, they don't know that many musical instruments are being used or what these instruments look or sound like. Listen to music with your child. Examine pictures of different instruments and identify their sounds.

- Help your child make simple soundmakers. Use materials that you find around the house. Put beans or rice in a plastic egg. Hang bells on a ribbon or a piece of string. Use two wooden spoons to hit together.

- Play simple listening games like Simon Says and Giant Steps.

When talking with your child, be aware of the following situations that have a negative influence on the development of listening skills:

- Repeating instructions several times encourages careless listening. A child who misses the instruction the first or second time knows it will be given a third or fourth time. A child who learns that you do not continue repeating instructions will learn to listen carefully.

- When having a serious discussion, don't try to compete with the television set, record player, or radio. Turn off or shut out distracting noises and be sure the child listens to what you are saying.

ABOUT THE ACTIVITIES

What's That I Hear provides activities that parents, caregivers, and teachers may use to develop and refine listening skills. These activities are not meant to be sequential. They may be used with large or small groups or with a single child, depending on each child's needs and abilities.

For ease in locating an activity appropriate for a particular group or scheduling need, the activities are divided into categories. A great deal of overlapping occurs between categories. For example, Word Pictures and Music Pictures are in the section on Being Creative, although they are based on story-telling and musical activities respectively. Dance to Directions is in the Music and Movement Section, although it also relates to Following Directions.

The activities list materials needed and detail the procedures to follow. At the end of each lesson, questions or statements are suggested to elicit follow-up conversation about the activity.

Listening for Sounds

1 • A LISTENING WALK

Skill Development: 1. Critical listening
2. Purposeful listening

Materials: None

Procedure: Plan a listening walk. Decide in advance what sound you will listen for such as birds, frogs, dogs, airplanes, or children's voices. Have the children count the number or call out the name each time that particular sound is heard.

2 • HERE OH WHERE?

Skill Development: 1. Auditory perception
2. Auditory discrimination
3. Critical listening

Materials: Key ring, metal objects, and soft objects

Procedure: Show the children the objects. Tell them you are going to move one of the objects and you want them to guess where. The children close their eyes and put their heads on their desks. Make noises as you walk around the room and when you put the object down. Then return to the front of the class and tell the children to open their eyes. Ask the children who think they know where you placed the object to hold up their hands so you can call on them.

Conversation: Hard objects and soft objects make different sounds when they are laid down or dropped. What are some reasons for these different sounds?

3 • I CAN LISTEN

Skill Development: 1. Listening for information
2. Auditory appreciation

Materials: Chalkboard and chalk or experience chart and marker

Procedure: The children pretend they have paper sacks over their heads and cannot see. They close their eyes tightly, listen to all the normal classroom sounds, and identify as many as possible, calling them out while you write them down. Who can identify the most sounds? This game may also be played on the playground where the children can walk around.

Conversation: How difficult would it be if you could not see? Does being able to hear help you when you cannot see?

4 • PAIRS OF SOUNDS

Skill Development: 1. Listening for information
                                   2. Auditory discrimination

Materials: Identical pairs of colored plastic eggs, egg carton, groups of small like objects such as marbles, rice, beans, and pebbles

Procedure: Find two identical eggs. Put a few identical items in both eggs. Repeat with the remaining pairs of eggs and objects, putting the same objects in identical eggs. The children shake the eggs carefully and listen to the sounds they make. When two eggs sound alike, the child places them side-by-side in the carton.

Conversation: Some things sound alike and some things sound different. What made some eggs sound alike and others sound different? What happens when you shake real eggs?

5 • SLEEP TIGHT

Skill Development:
1. Listening for problem solving
2. Critical listening

Materials:
A "white-noise" sound machine used for sleeping, a pie pan, and a hammer

Procedure:
Use this activity during the rest period. After the children have rested quietly for about five minutes, say in a low voice that they are going to hear two sounds and must decide which sound they want for rest time. First, bang the pie pan with the hammer several times. Then plug in the sound machine and let the children listen to white noise. Ask which sound they prefer.

Conversation:
Did the sound of banging on the pie pan help you rest?

Was the sound machine something that helped you rest?

Different sounds are used for different reasons. For what reasons do you think these two sounds are used?

6 • MARCHING AROUND THE ROOM

Skill Development: 1. Following directions
2. Critical listening (cause and effect)

Materials: None

Procedure: Tell the children that you are going to teach them to march. Ask them to stand in rows four abreast. Tell them to start with the left foot and follow your commands, "Left, right, left." After they have learned to march, tell them you will give two commands while they are marching. One will be to march loudly (stomping), and the other will be to march quietly (tiptoeing). March loudly for a few minutes and then march quietly. Ask the children what will happen if they march loudly in the classroom during other activities or at other times of the day. (They will disturb other children or other classes.)

Conversation: What differences did you hear in the two kinds of marching?
Which type of marching can you do inside and which should you do outside? Why?
What other things should be done outside because of the noise?

7 • NIGHT SOUNDS

Skill Development:
1. Auditory discrimination
2. Auditory association
3. Listening for information
4. Creative listening

Materials:
Tape recorder, blank recording tape, heavy-duty extension cord, experience chart, and markers

In advance of the class, the children take turns taking home the tape recorder and extension cord. The tape recorder is placed at the very back of their yards in the evening, and left running for an hour. If it is not possible to send the tape recorder home with the children, record in the yards of your friends and neighbors.

Procedure:
Each time the tape recorder is returned to the class, the children listen to it. Write every sound they recognize on the experience chart. After several evenings have been recorded on the chart, compare the sounds heard in different locations. Match as many common sounds as possible.

Conversation:
Different houses and neighborhoods have different sounds.
What were some common sounds?
What sounds such as a dog barking were found in only certain backyards? Why?

8 • SITTING-DOWN SOUNDS

Skill Development: 1. Creative listening
2. Auditory memory
3. Auditory association

Materials: None

Procedure: With the children seated in a circle, explain that it is not always necessary to get up and run around to make noise. It is possible to make noises while sitting down and without talking. Challenge the children to see what noises they can make without moving around the room and without talking. Ask each child to make a noise that no one else has made.

Examples:

Shuffling feet	Clicking tongue
Snapping fingers	Hissing
Whistling	Clapping
Humming	Coughing
Tapping fingers	Rubbing hands together

Conversation: When would you want to make a noise without talking? (To get attention.)
Is it possible to sit for a long time without making some noise? Let's try it.

9 • SOUND WHEEL

Skill Development: 1. Auditory association
2. Creative listening
3. Auditory appreciation

Materials: Cardboard, scissors, crayons, and a brad

Prepare a sound wheel as illustrated below. Cut a circle and an arrow from cardboard. Divide the circle into six sections and write the name or draw a picture of a sound-making item in each section. Punch a hole in the arrow and wheel and fasten the arrow to the wheel with a brad. Turn the arrow a few times until it spins freely.

Procedure: The children take turns spinning the arrow and making the sound of the item indicated by the pointer.

Conversation: Do you hear most of these sounds every day? Do non-living things make sounds just like living things?

10 • WHAT'S THAT I HEAR?

Skill Development: 1. Auditory perception
2. Auditory association
3. Auditory discrimination
4. Listening for problem solving

Materials: Objects that make sounds such as a bell, paper to crumple, sticks to hit together, a horn, a book to drop, and water to sip

Procedure: Ask the children to close their eyes and put their heads down on their desks while you make various sounds with the objects. The children try to imagine how you are making the sounds and raise their hands when they think they know. When most of the children have raised their hands, let them see if they were correct.

Conversation: Some things sound like other things and some sound different.

11 • MAKING SOUNDS

Skill Development: 1. Auditory discrimination
2. Auditory association
3. Critical listening
4. Creative listening

Materials: None

Procedure: With the children seated, explain that they are going to play a game of making sounds. Each child takes a turn standing in front of the group and making a sound. The other children try to identify the sound. If they cannot think of a sound that something makes, they may make any sound and describe an imaginary object that makes this sound.

Conversation: Can you think of things that make no sound?
Can you make up a creature and give it a sound?

12 • WHAT WAS TAKEN?

Skill Development: 1. Auditory discrimination
2. Auditory association

Materials: Zipper, bell, key ring with keys, paper to crumple, and other small objects

Procedure: Place the objects on a table. Ask one child to look at the objects for a minute or two. Have the child turn away from the table. Remove one object from the table, make a sound with it, and then hold it behind your back. Ask the child to turn around and tell you which object is missing.

Conversation: Does knowing the sound an object makes help you remember the object?
When you hear a sound, can you visualize what is making it?

13 • I KNOW THAT SOUND

Skill Development: 1. Auditory discrimination
2. Purposeful listening

Materials: Bell, keys, zipper, comb, ruler, and other small objects

Procedure: Place all the items on a table. Be sure every child has the opportunity to explore the objects and the noises they make. Ask the children to close their eyes and place their heads on their desks. Make noises with each object and call upon different children to identify the objects without raising their heads.

Conversation: In what ways do some of the objects sound alike?
In what ways do they they sound different?

14 • QUIET TIME

Skill Development:
1. Purposeful listening
2. Auditory discrimination
3. Following directions

Materials:
Wall clock, chalkboard and chalk, or experience chart and markers

Procedure:
Tell the children to be as quiet as possible for five minutes. Show them where the hand on the wall clock will be in five minutes. Ask them to listen to all the different sounds they can hear while everyone is quiet. At the end of five minutes, ask each child to tell you a sound heard during the quiet time. Write the different sounds on the chalkboard or experience chart.

Conversation:
How are sounds different?
What sounds do you like to hear or dislike to hear?
Why are sounds different?
Why do some things make sounds?
Why are some sounds more important than others?

15 • WHISPERING TIME

Skill Development: 1. Purposeful listening
2. Reactions to sounds

Materials: A wall clock

Procedure: Explain that you are going to set aside 15 minutes of the day when no one will be allowed to talk above a whisper. It may be necessary to practice whispering before you begin. Some children will forget during the allotted time. Mark the time with tape on the clock to help the children remember.

Conversation: Does it sound different in the room when everybody whispers?
What must you do to hear and understand? (Listen closely.)
Can you name times when it is better to whisper than talk out loud? (In church, during rest time, at home when someone is sleeping.)

Rhyming and
Word Fun

16 • HEY DIDDLE DIDDLE

Skill Development: 1. Rhyming
2. Creative listening

Materials: Book of nursery rhymes

Procedure: Ask the children to recite the nursery rhyme "Hey Diddle Diddle" in unison. Then ask them to help you think of ways to change the rhyme in the first line. Make up rhymes and let the children supply the missing word. Throughout the day, ask the children to use these rhymes when appropriate.

Examples:
Hey diddle diddle, we cook on a ____ (griddle).
Hey diddle dock, I lost my ____ (sock).
Hey diddle dee, my dog has a ____ (flea).
Hey diddle doo, where's my shoe?
Hey diddle dack, it's time for a snack.

Conversation: How can you have fun with words?
When does a sentence make sense and when is it nonsense?

17 • ICK THE CHICK

Skill Development: 1. Purposeful listening
2. Rhyming

Materials: Egg cartons, scissors, glue, black paper, and cotton balls

Procedure: Each child makes a chick as shown in the illustration below. When the children have finished, introduce the following poem:

> I am Ick the Chick.
> Pick me up, I will not stick.
> I don't drink coffee, I don't drink tea,
> Find a word that rhymes with me.

Use the poem to point out rhyming words. Read nursery rhymes to the children, occasionally leaving out a rhyming word and helping the children supply it. Help the children make up their own rhymes to fit the pattern of Ick the Chick.

Conversation: Why do some words sound alike?
What are some other rhyming words you can think of?

Skill Development: 1. Rhyming
2. Auditory memory

Materials: List of rhyming words and non-rhyming words

Procedure: Discuss how rhyming words sound alike and give examples. Explain to the children that they are going to listen to you read three words. Two of the words will rhyme and one will not. The children will take turns repeating the word that does not rhyme. All the children will not be successful at first. Work with them individually until all have had a successful experience.

Conversation: What do rhyming words sound like?
How do you listen for rhyme?

19 • RHYME AROUND A CIRCLE

Skill Development: 1. Auditory discrimination
                        2. Rhyming

Materials: None

Procedure: With the children in a circle, select one child to be *It.* That child stands in the middle of the circle, calls out a word (like "mouse"), points to a child in the circle, and calls out that child's name. If the child called upon says a rhyming word ("house" to rhyme with "mouse"), *It* calls out the same word ("mouse") again, points to another child, and calls that child by name. A child who cannot respond with a rhyming word becomes *It.* In the beginning of the game, you may supply the words for *It.* No child should be called upon twice before all have a turn.

Conversation: How do words sound alike?
                   Why do words sound alike?
                   Do some words look alike and sound different? Why?

20 • SOUNDS LIKE

Skill Development:
1. Rhyming
2. Purposeful listening
3. Auditory discrimination
4. Auditory perception
5. Auditory appreciation

Materials:
Magazines, scissors, glue, and construction paper

Procedure:
Each child finds a picture of an animal in a magazine, cuts it out, and mounts it on construction paper. Display the pictures on the chalk ledge. Select a picture without telling which one. Make up a short poem to help the children identify the animal through rhyming words. The child who supplies the missing word points to the correct picture.

Examples:
I jump around and dance a jig
I don't move fast because I'm a _____ (pig).

I chew my bone under a log.
I'm a fat and lazy _____ (dog).

If "tweet tweet" is what you heard,
Then you know I'm a little _____ (bird).

I like to curl up on a mat.
You'll hear me purr because I'm a _____ (cat).

I like to scurry through the house
And eat lots of cheese because I'm a _____ (mouse).

I run a race and complete the course.
A cowboy loves his faithful _____ (horse).

Conversation:
Do words that rhyme have a lot of the same letters?
How do you know when words rhyme?

21 • OPPOSITES

Skill Development:
1. Listening for problem solving
2. Creative listening
3. Critical listening

Materials: None

Procedure: Explain to the children what is meant by *opposite*. Give examples such as *hot* and *cold, big* and *little*. Ask the children to think of pairs of words that mean the opposite of each other. When they seem to understand the concept, tell them you are going to say some things that mean the opposite, but you are going to leave out a word. Can they guess the right word?

Examples:

At night it is dark.   During the day it is _____ .

The window is open.   The door is _____ .
The desk is clean.   The floor is _____ .
The ruler is straight.   My hair is _____ .
This book is old.   The chalk is _____ .
Lemons are sour.   Candy is _____ .

Conversation: What is the meaning of opposite?
How many opposites do you know?

22 • WHERE IS MY MOUTH?

Skill Development: 1. Purposeful listening
2. Critical listening

Materials: Prepare in advance a number of correct and absurd statements involving the mouth and eating. See the examples of absurd statements below.

Procedure: Ask the children to tell you when they hear you say something absurd. Read a series of correct statements and insert an absurd statement. After the children have identified the absurdity, ask them why they think it was absurd.

Examples of absurd statements:
John took off his shoe so he could drink a glass of water.
Joey used his toothbrush to wash the car.
Sara wanted an apple so she peeled an orange.
Lisa washed her hair with whipped cream.
Micky loved the spaghetti so he dumped it in his pocket.

Conversation: Why do we think some statements are foolish?
Where is your mouth?
Is everybody's mouth in the same place?
What do we use our mouths for?

23 • WHOSE RIDDLE IS THAT?

Skill Development:
1. Auditory discrimination
2. Auditory association
3. Listening for problem solving

Materials: Tape recorder and blank tapes

Procedure: Young children enjoy asking riddles. Have each child record a riddle. With the children seated facing the tape recorder, play back a riddle. Ask one child to identify the voice. If the identification is correct, the child tries to guess the answer to the riddle. If the identification is incorrect, another child has the chance to guess. Be sure each riddle is answered correctly before moving on.

Conversation: How do voices sound different when they are recorded?
What else can we use a tape recorder for?

24 • WHICH IS SILLY?

Skill Development: 1. Auditory association
2. Critical listening

Materials: None

Procedure: Explain that you are going to say two sentences. One of the sentences will make sense and one will be silly. Ask the children to listen carefully and tell you which sentence is silly.

Examples:
When it's cold I wear a coat.
When it's cold I wear a swimsuit.

The little fish swam away.
The little bird swam away.

Conversation: What makes each silly sentence silly?

"THE LITTLE FISH SWAM AWAY" or "THE LITTLE BIRD SWAM AWAY"?

THE LITTLE BIRD!

Clues and Descriptions

25 • MATCHING DESCRIPTIONS

Skill Development: 1. Creative listening
2. Auditory association
3. Auditory appreciation
4. Purposeful listening

Materials: Magazines, catalogs, scissors, glue, half sheets of construction paper, and a basket or box

Procedure: The children look through the magazines and catalogs to find pictures of objects that make noise. They cut out the pictures and mount them on construction paper. Collect the pictures and put them in a basket or box. Ask the children to come up one at a time and draw a picture from the basket. The children look at their pictures and, without making the associated sound, describe the object.

Conversation: What are the actual sounds the items make? Why is it hard to describe a sound-making object without actually making the sound?

Skill Development: 1. Purposeful listening
2. Listening for problem solving

Materials: None

Procedure: The children stand in a circle and choose one person (Child 1) to stand in the center of the circle and be *It.* Child 1 asks Child 2, "Have you seen my lost child?" Child 2 asks, "What is your child wearing?" Child 1 describes a feature of a third child, "My child is wearing red socks." Child 2 identifies Child 3 or says, "No, I haven't seen your child." Child 1 then chooses a fourth child and begins the same conversation, describing another feature of Child 3: "My child is wearing a green sweater. This continues until Child 3 is identified.

Conversation: What should a lost child do?
Who should a lost child look for?

27 • I'M THINKING OF . . .

Skill Development: 1. Purposeful listening
2. Critical listening

Materials: None

Procedure: Give clues about the object you are thinking about and let the children try to guess what that object is.

Examples:
I'm thinking of something that birds eat. (Worms, seeds)
I'm thinking of something you wear when swimming. (Goggles, swimsuit)

Try to make statements that have more than one correct response. After the children have responded to several statements, divide them into small groups and let them play the game themselves.

Conversation: Some information can apply to more than one answer.
Sometimes only one answer is correct.

28 • DESCRIBE IT!

Skill Development:
1. Auditory discrimination
2. Purposeful listening

Materials:
A pillow case, small items such as crayons, rocks, a ball, cloth, a comb, a seashell, and beans

Procedure:
Put all the small items in the pillow case. The children sit on the floor and take turns reaching into the bag, selecting one item without looking, and describing it by the way it feels. The other children try to determine what the item is from the description. The children who think they know, hold up their hands and keep them up until the child describing the object also knows, calls out the name of the object, and shows it to the class. How many children were correct with their guess?

Conversation:
How can you describe something by just feeling it? (Smooth, rough, split, bumpy, round, corners, holes, small, sticky, hard, soft)

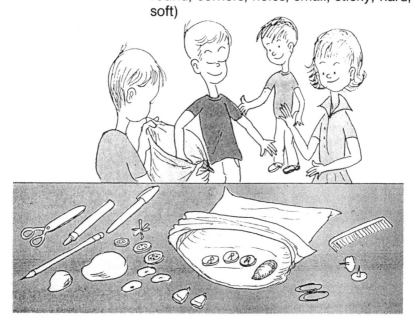

29 • SHOW AND TELL

Skill Development: 1. Purposeful listening
2. Critical Listening
3. Asking questions
4. Listening to seek correct answers to questions

Materials: The day before, ask the children to bring something from home in a paper sack. They may bring a small stuffed animal, a picture, an apple, a spoon, a book, or a toy

Procedure: Instead of participating in a regular Show and Tell, the children take turns describing or giving hints about what is in their sacks. The other children try to guess what is in the sack. Encourage the children to ask questions in complete sentences.

Conversation: What is a question?
Why do you ask questions?

30 • HOW DO THEY FEEL?

Skill Development:
1. Auditory discrimination
2. Critical listening
3. Listening for problem solving
4. Auditory association

Materials:
Three pictures of faces that clearly show emotion

Procedure:
Display the pictures on the chalk ledge or wall. Make a few statements about each picture without using the word for the emotion being expressed.

Example:
This is Tony. Tony's mother gave him an ice cream cone. Tony loves ice cream, but the ice cream fell out of the cone.

After listening to a description of all three pictures, can the children identify the emotions being expressed. Ask how the person in the picture feels.

Conversation:
Why did you choose this picture?
Is it all right to show emotion?

Being
Creative

31 • MAKE UP A STORY

Skill Development: 1. Association of sounds and past experiences
2. Auditory association
3. Creative listening

Materials: Tape recorder and tape of recorded sounds

Procedure: Before the activity, record several sounds on tape, spacing them at various intervals. Sounds could include buzzing, water running, phone ringing, paper crumpling, and a dog barking. The children listen to the tape and try to construct a story based on the sounds they hear.

Conversation: How sounds are different depends on what is making the sound.

Skill Development:
1. Purposeful listening
2. Critical listening
3. Following directions

Materials:
Rubber bands, packages of round mint or fruit candy with holes through the centers, sticks of gum, craft sticks, stick candy or small rolls of mints

Procedure:
Give each child one rubber band, two round candies, a stick of gum, a craft stick, and a stick candy or roll of mints. Ask the children to use the items to make something that is used for transportation. *Give the children time* to construct their objects. Accept and compliment all their efforts. If children need directions, tell them to follow these instructions: Pass a rubber band through the holes of two round candies; loop each end of the rubber band over an opposite end of a stick of gum; place the craft stick between the candies and under the gum to make an airplane. Encourage the children to share their vehicles.

Conversation:
Many different things may be made from the same materials. How else could you use these materials to make things?
How can you improve the things you've already made?

Skill Development: 1. Auditory perception
2. Auditory appreciation
3. Purposeful listening
4. Following directions

Materials: Hammer, piano wire, and for each "telephone" set, two small nails and two tin cans each with one end removed and no rough edges

Procedure: With the hammer and a nail, punch a hole in the center of one can. Thread the wire through the can from the outside. Tie the wire around the nail to keep it from slipping out. Repeat with the remaining can and nail. Stretch the wire tight and explain that the children will use it as a telephone for giving directions. One child is the "direction giver" and speaks into one of the cans. Another child, the listener, holds the second can over her or his ear. The "direction giver" gives a command such as "Hop like a bunny." The listener carries out the command and the other children try to guess what the command was. Let each child have a turn using the telephone.

Conversation: How can you hear with this telephone? Could you make a party line?

34 • MAKING MASKS

Skill Development: 1. Auditory association
2. Auditory discrimination
3. Creative listening

Materials: A large paper sack for each child, crayons, and scissors.

Prepare in advance a paper-sack mask of a cow's face for yourself to wear.

Procedure: Put your mask over your head in front of the children. How many of the children know that a cow says "moo?" Ask the children to make masks for themselves. Let the children create their own masks. Show them how you cut out holes for the eyes and mouth and decorated your mask. When the masks are finished, the children take turns standing in front of the class wearing their masks. The other children try to guess the sound that is associated with the mask. If nobody guesses, the child makes the appropriate sound.

Conversation: How did you know what sound to associate with the mask?

We often associate a sound with an object without hearing the sound. For example, we look at a telephone and know it will ring. What else do we look at and know what kind of sound it makes?

35 • TELEVISION PROGRAMS

Skill Development: 1. Auditory appreciation
2. Creative listening

Materials: A large cardboard box with one side removed and a 24-inch square cut out of the opposite side, markers or paints, cards numbered 1 through 13, and tape or pins

Procedure: Place the box on a table with the cut-out square facing the class. Tell the children to pretend it is a television set, and ask them to draw or paint dials and selectors on the box. Tape or pin a numbered card on half the children in the class. The children with the numbers stand behind the box while the other children stand in front of the box. The children in front of the box take turns pretending to turn the selector to different channels. While selecting the channel, the child says, "I want to watch channel four." The child wearing the number 4 card stands behind the TV as if appearing on a program and talks, sings, recites, or tells a story. Be sure all the children have a chance to be "on TV."

Conversation: How did each child sound?
How were their voices different?

36 • PRETENDING

Skill Development: 1. Auditory appreciation
2. Mental imagry
3. Listening to seek correct answers to questions

Materials: Dress-up outfits including both men's and women's clothing

Procedure: The children take turns, one or two at a time, dressing up like someone they know without giving any names or categories. Ask the other children if they can understand what the portrayed characters look like and act like.

Conversation: Everybody is different. What is different about you?
Can you describe this difference?

37 • PUPPET PLAY

Skill Development: 1. Following directions
2. Critical listening

Materials: Pencil, white or tan flannel, scissors, large needles, yarn, and markers.

Make a puppet to introduce to the children. Draw the puppet's shape, as shown below, on two one-foot square pieces of flannel. Cut out the shapes and sew them together, leaving the bottom open. Add a face, yarn hair, and buttons as desired.

Procedure: Give each child two one-foot square pieces of flannel with the puppet shape drawn on them. Scissors, large needles, yarn, and markers should be available. Hold up your puppet and talk to the children. Tell them that you are lonesome being the only puppet in the room, but they can make a puppet to keep you company. They are to listen carefully and you will tell them how to do it. Let your puppet give directions as the children cut out the puppet shapes, place one on top of the other, and sew them together with yarn. Faces, yarn hair, and buttons may be added. When they are finished, the roomful of puppets can talk together.

Conversation: Can puppets really talk?
Who talks for the puppets?
How does the puppet know what to say?

Skill Development: 1. Following directions
2. Critical listening
3. Purposeful listening

Materials: Heavy paper, crayons, scissors, glue and tape or staples, and several large rabbit-ear patterns (see the illustration below)

Procedure: Pass out paper, crayons, scissors, and glue. Explain to the children that they are going to make rabbit ears and then they are going to listen with them like rabbits do. Pass out the rabbit-ear patterns for the children to trace, cut out, and color. While the children are doing this, cut a two-inch headband for each child. Wrap a headband around each child's head and tape or staple it to fit. Show the children how to attach the rabbit ears to the headband. Tell the children that when you say "Rabbit," they put on their ears, hop like a rabbit, and find something to listen to very closely.

Conversation: Why do rabbits have big ears?
How do they use them?
Do their big ears help them hear better?
How do our ears help us hear?

39 • WORD PICTURES

Skill Development:
1. Critical listening
2. Purposeful listening
3. Following directions
4. Mental manipulation of words

Materials:
A book of children's poems or stories, large heavy paper, pencils, and crayons

Procedure:
Read a poem or a story to the children. Then tell the children to listen carefully while you re-read a section that vividly describes a scene. Ask the children to draw a picture about what you have just read. Let the children show their pictures to the class and talk about them.

Conversation:
The story was the same but all the pictures are different.
Why are some things alike in the pictures?
Why are some things different?

40 • MUSIC PICTURES

Skill Development: 1. Auditory appreciation
2. Listening for enjoyment
3. Association of sounds and past experiences

Materials: Record player, records, crayons, and paper

Procedure: Play the records and ask the children to draw colored pictures while listening to the music. Change the music frequently, being sure to use different types of music. Ask the children how it makes them want to draw. Encourage them to portray what they feel. It is the process that is important, not the product.

Conversation: How does the music make you feel?
What does it make you want to do?

Stories, Poems,
and Nursery Rhymes

41 • STORY TAPES

Skill Development: Auditory appreciation

Materials: Tape recorder, blank recording tapes, and children's stories

Procedure: Record several of the children's favorite stories. Provide opportunities in the listening center or reading center for the children to listen to the tapes.

Conversation: How could you draw a picture to show what happened in the story?
How could you act out the story?

Skill Development: 1. Auditory appreciation
2. Awareness of language patterns

Materials: Book of children's stories

Procedure: Set aside a period every day for story time. During this time, read a story to the children for their enjoyment. Children may have favorites that they want to hear several times over. Unless there is a specific purpose, avoid reading the same story twice in one day. Follow story time with conversation and a related activity.

Conversation: What did the characters in the story do?
Did the characters in the story paint pictures, take a walk, or prepare a basket for a picnic?
What are some things we can do now that the story told about?

43 • SOLVE THE PROBLEM

Skill Development:
1. Critical listening
2. Listening for problem solving
3. Auditory appreciation

Materials:
A book of nursery rhymes

Procedure:
Most nursery rhymes contain the basis for a problem. For example, if four and twenty blackbirds are baked in a pie and then fly away, how can you get them back? How can Humpty-Dumpty be put back together again? What can we do about Jack's broken crown? Read these rhymes to the children and ask what can be done to solve each problem. Accept all answers because there are no correct ones. Creativity is fostered by the acceptance of divergent answers.

Conversation:
Did these rhymes really happen?
What is the difference between fantasy and reality?
What is fantasy?
What is reality?

44 • FLANNEL BOARD FUN

Skill Development: 1. Auditory appreciation
2. Listening for enjoyment
3. Creative listening

Materials: Flannel board and cutout characters

Procedure: Tell a flannel board story to the class for their enjoyment. After the story, leave the characters and the flannel board out for a few days so the children may manipulate the cutouts and tell their own versions of the story.

Conversation: Which character in the story is your favorite?
Did you like the way the story ended?
Do you have a better ending?

45 • BEFORE AND AFTER

Skill Development: 1. Purposeful listening
2. Rhyming

Materials: Nursery rhymes or children's poetry

Procedure: Read a nursery rhyme or a poem to the children at least twice. Ask the children questions about the action in the rhyme and about what happened to the characters. It may be necessary to read the poem a third time. It may be helpful to use a flannel board or illustration to recreate the sequence of events.

Conversation: What do you think happened to the characters before the rhyme?
What do you think happened to them after the rhyme?

46 • ENJOYING FABLES

Skill Development: 1. Auditory Appreciation
2. Listening for information

Materials: A book of fables for young children

Procedure: Read simple fables to the children for their listening enjoyment. Have the children take turns telling what each fable is trying to teach.

Conversation: What is a fable?
Can you make up a fable to share with the group?

47 • PEACEFUL POEMS

Skill Development: 1. Auditory appreciation
2. Awareness of rhyme

Materials: Book of children's poems containing selections about nature

Procedure: Read several nature poems and let the children comment without your questions or explanations. After the children have commented, discuss how poetry is used to create moods and feelings. From time to time, read the poems again for their enjoyment and further appreciation.

Conversation: Everyone has feelings. What are some of your feelings?
Feelings need to be expressed in acceptable ways. How do you express them?

" Wynken, Blynken, and Nod one night
    Sailed off in a wooden shoe,—
  Sailed on a river of crystal light
  Into a sea of dew. "

Skill Development: 1. Critical listening
2. Auditory memory
3. Purposeful listening

Materials: Tape recorder, blank recording tape, and three children's stories.

Prepare a tape in advance by taping the beginning of one story as you read it. After a few minutes, change to the middle of the second story. After another few minutes, change to the end of the third story. On the tape, the beginning of one story, the middle of another, and the end of a third will all run together without any identification.

Procedure: Assemble the children for story time. Tell them that today you are going to play a story on tape for them. Ask them to listen closely so they can re-tell the story after they have heard the tape. When the tape is finished, ask the children if they can retell the story.

Conversation: Why was what you heard not a story? (A story must be a certain sequence.)
Was what you heard a sequence or a disorder?
When did you notice that the story was not in sequence?

49 • ACTING OUT STORIES

Skill Development: 1. Auditory discrimination
2. Creative listening
3. Purposeful listening

Materials: A children's story that will be easy to role play

Procedure: Before reading the story, tell the children to listen carefully because you are going to ask them to act it out. Then read the story. If it is short, read it again. Ask for volunteers to role play the story. Give assistance only if the children ask for it.

Conversation: Why is listening carefully to different parts of the story important?
Who do you like to play in the story and why?

50 • HOW DO YOU FEEL?

Skill Development: 1. Auditory association
                              2. Auditory appreciation

Materials: An illustrated story, nursery rhyme, or poem that is likely to arouse the child's emotions

Procedure: Read the selection to the children and allow time for them to study the pictures. Ask different children how different parts of what you read made them feel. For example, if you read "Jack and Jill," the children could relate to Jack and Jill falling and to Jack's injury. Another example is "Billy Goats Gruff." The children could relate to the hunger, fear of the troll, the fight, and the triumph of getting over the bridge.

Conversation: Why do certain things we see or do make us feel certain ways?
Is it okay to be angry or scared?

51 • WHAT'S THE TITLE

Skill Development: 1. Listening for information
2. Auditory memory
3. Auditory appreciation

Materials: Several children's stories and poems

Procedure: Tell the children you are going to read a story or poem to them, but you are not going to tell them the title. Ask them to listen carefully, and if they have heard the story or poem before, to call out the title. If the children do not recognize the selection, ask them to make up a title that would fit.

Conversation: Why do you think a certain story or poem has a particular title?
When you didn't know the real title of the story or poem, why did you select the title you did?

Skill Development: 1. Critical listening
2. Listening for information

Materials: A familiar children's story

Procedure: Gather the children for story time. Explain that they are to listen very carefully because you might make a mistake. If you make a mistake, the children are to call it to your attention and correct it.

Examples:
And when Goldilocks looked on the table, she found three bowls of chili.

Conversation: Are all stories real?
What are stories for?
What are some favorite stories?

Skill Development: 1. Rhyming
2. Critical listening
3. Purposeful listening

Materials: A book of nursery rhymes

Procedure: Read nursery rhymes to the children. Encourage them to say the rhymes with you. Have the children act out simple rhymes and draw pictures about them.

Conversation: Who are the characters in the rhymes and what are they doing?

These nursery rhymes were written a long time ago. If they were written today, how would they be different?

What is fantasy?

What is reality?

Skill Development: 1. Auditory perception
2. Auditory memory
3. Purposeful listening
4. Auditory discrimination

Materials: Tape recorder, blank recording tape, and children's stories

In advance, record several stories on tape.

Procedure: In class, give the child the book to "read" while listening to the taped story. Encourage the children to talk about a story or retell it into the recorder. When everyone has recorded, play the tape back so the children can listen to themselves. They may also dramatize the stories or draw pictures of what they hear.

Conversation: Sounds can be recorded and stored.
People sound different on tape.

55 • OUCH! THAT'S HOT

Skill Development: 1. Auditory appreciation
2. Purposeful listening
3. Following directions

Materials: A book about Goldilocks and the three bears, grocery sacks for making masks, three empty bowls, and spoons

Procedure: Read the story to the children. Then ask them to act out the parts of the story. Show the children how to make bear masks from paper sacks and to decorate them to look like Mama Bear, Papa Bear, Baby Bear, and Goldilocks. Have them act out the story while wearing the masks. To further extend the activity and make it more realistic, cook oatmeal and use it for a prop.

Conversation: Can you retell the story or parts of the story? How should we (did we) organize or plan the play?

Following Directions

56 • COMMAND RELAY

Skill Development: 1. Purposeful listening
2. Auditory memory
3. Following directions

Materials: Pairs of various objects such as 2 hats, 2 blocks, and 2 crayons

Procedure: Divide the children into two relay lines. In front of each line, place three objects the children can pick up at the same time. Give a series of commands and the first child on each team will carry out the commands and run to the back of the line. Then you will give the next two children another series of commands.

Example:
Put the hat under my desk. Put the block on the windowsill. Put the crayon on the chalk ledge.

The children must follow the directions in the order you give them. Vary the difficulty of the commands according to the abilities of the children. Continue until all children have participated.

Conversation: Is it hard to remember a series of commands in the proper order?
What is sequence?
Will listening carefully help you remember proper sequence?

57 • MEMORY RELAY

Skill Development: 1. Auditory memory
2. Following directions
3. Purposeful listening

Materials: Pairs of various objects such as 2 chairs, 2 hats, and 2 mittens

Procedure: Divide the children into two relay lines. A few feet in front of each line, place three or four objects. Give a series of commands. The first child on each team will carry out the commands and run back to tap the next two players who will perform the same tasks.

Example:
   Walk around the chair. Put on the hat. Take off the hat. Step over the mitten.

Continue the relay until all the children have had a turn.

Conversation: How do you listen to directions?
What do you do when you have a lot of directions to follow?

58 • IN THE BOX

Skill Development:
1. Following directions
2. Auditory memory
3. Listening for information
4. Awareness of spatial relations

Materials:
A large cardboard box for a child to sit in

Procedure:
Place the box on the floor and tell the children that each one will have a turn following directions. Select the first child and give a series of directions. Allow the child time to complete one direction before going on to the next.

Example:
Sit in front of the box. Stand beside the box. Stand behind the box. Sit inside the box. Stand under the box. (The child must decide to lift up the box to follow this last command.)

Conversation:
Let's talk about words like *behind, in front of, beside, inside,* and *under.*

59 • RIGHT OR LEFT?

Skill Development: 1. Auditory memory
2. Listening for information
3. Following directions

Materials: None

Procedure: The children stand in a circle with some distance .between them. Tell them you are going to give directions for using their right and left hands and they are to do as you say. If some children are having trouble with the right-left concept, tie a string around their right wrists. Then give a series of directions, allowing the children time to respond to each one.

Examples:
Touch your nose with your right hand.
Put your left hand on your chest.
Touch your right elbow with your left hand.
Put your right hand on top of your head.

Conversation: When do you use your right hand?
When do you use your left hand?
How many parts of your body can you name?
How can you listen carefully to directions?

60 • DO AS I SAY

Skill Development: 1. Following directions
2. Auditory memory
3. Critical listening
4. Purposeful listening

Materials: None

Procedure: With the children seated, give one child at a time a series of commands to follow.

Examples:
Marcia, jump once, hop to the door, knock three times, and return to your seat.

Rob, tiptoe around the room, touch every other child, sit back in your seat.

The directions may become more difficult as the activity progresses.

Conversation: How do you follow directions?
How many directions at a time can you remember?

61 • CATCH A PLANE

Skill Development: 1. Following directions
2. Auditory discrimination

Materials: A chair for each child

Procedure: Arrange the chairs in a circle with a child sitting in each chair. Explain to the children that they are at the airport waiting to board their plane. Select one child as the caller. When the caller calls out "Everybody to the right" or "Everybody to the left," each child shifts in the direction named to the next chair. If one of the children makes a mistake, the caller can grab the seat and the child who lost the seat becomes the caller.

Conversation: Following directions can be difficult.
Sometimes we get left and right confused.

62 • TRAVELING CAT

Skill Development: 1. Following directions
2. Purposeful listening

Materials: A small stuffed toy cat

Procedure: Tell the children that they are going to play Traveling Cat. Explain that you will give a series of directions asking different children to put the cat in certain places in the room. You will give the directions once only so they must listen carefully. The children should act in the order the directions are given. Be sure all the children have a turn.

Examples:
John, put the cat on the blocks.
Mary, put the cat beside the wastebasket.
George, put the cat in the doll bed.

Conversation: What must you do to pay close attention when someone talks or gives directions?

63 • TELEPHONE ANSWERING

Skill Development:
1. Purposeful listening
2. Auditory memory

Materials:
Toy telephones with battery pack or phones supplied by local telephone company

Procedure:
Talk with the children about the proper way to answer the telephone. Have them practice answering the telephone, taking messages, and relaying messages to others. They can pretend to be talking to a relative, a department store clerk, a neighbor, or some other person. The child answers the telephone correctly, takes the message, hangs up the telephone, and relays the message correctly.

Conversation:
What are some correct ways to answer the telephone?
Who answers the telephone at your house?
Does anyone ever call you? Who?

Time Out
for a Game

64 • WHO AM I?

Skill Development:
1. Auditory discrimination
2. Auditory memory
3. Listening to seek correct answers to questions

Materials:
A blindfold

Procedure:
The children stand in a circle with one blindfolded child standing in the middle. One child in the circle makes the statement, "I am over here." The blindfolded child must point to the speaker and call her or him by name. If the identification was wrong, the blindfolded child may ask up to three questions which can be answered by only "Yes" or "No." If the child still can't be identified, another child calls, "I am over here." When identification is successful, the child who is identified changes places with the blindfolded child.

Conversation:
Why do different people have voices that sound different?
Is there a difference between little girls' voices and little boys' voices? Between women's and men's voices?

65 • TWENTY QUESTIONS

Skill Development: 1. Listening to seek correct answers to questions
2. Critical listening
3. Asking questions

Materials: None

Procedure: Each child takes a turn standing in front of the class, thinking of an object for the other children to guess by asking yes/no questions only. To begin, the child announces, "I am thinking about something in the room (in the street, to wear, to eat)." The other children take turns asking yes/no questions up to a total of 20 questions. Remind the children that they are trying to guess the object on the basis of previous questions and answers.

Conversation: It is hard to get information using questions that can be answered by only "Yes" or "No."
Sometimes you have to plan questions to get useful information.

Skill Development: 1. Auditory discrimination
2. Critical listening
3. Auditory memory

Materials: Pointer and alphabet cards posted on the walls

Procedure: Sing the following sentence to any tune, point to a letter of the alphabet, and call it out. The children whose name begins with the letter you call out must stand up. Be sure to give the children time to respond.

> If your name begins with the letter I call, please stand up. _____

Repeat the sentence in various tunes, pointing to and naming a different letter each time. Occasionally, repeat a letter previously named to keep the children alert.

Conversation: What other words start with the same letter as your name?
Do letters always have the same sound or do they sometimes sound different?

67 • GOSSIP

Skill Development:
1. Auditory memory
2. Auditory discrmination
3. Following directions

Materials: None

Procedure: With the children seated in a circle, whisper an instruction such as "Jump up and down" in the first child's ear. That child whispers the same instruction in the ear of the second child and so on around the circle. The last child will either act out the message or tell what was heard as the message.

Conversation: We should talk slowly and pay close attention to what others are saying.

68 • HOT AND COLD

Skill Development: 1. Listening for information
2. Critical listening
3. Auditory perception

Materials: Small items from the classroom

Procedure: The children take turns covering their eyes while another child hides an object. The child looking for the hidden object is guided to it by the way the other children clap their hands: The children begin by clapping their hands gently. As the searching child moves closer to the hidden object, the other children clap louder. If the searching child moves away from the object, the other children clap softer.

Conversation: What do the words *loud* and *soft* mean?
When are loud noises appropriate and when should children be quieter?

69 • BOUNCING BALLS

Skill Development: 1. Purposeful listening
2. Auditory discrimination
3. Auditory association

Materials: A basketball, a tennis ball, a softball, and a ping pong ball

Procedure: Let the children get acquainted with the balls and the sounds they make when they bounce. Then tell them that they will play a listening game with the balls. The children form a circle facing out. Stand in the center of the circle with the balls beside you. Select one of the balls without letting the children see which one and bounce it behind one child. That child guesses which ball you bounced. A child who guesses the right ball goes into the center of the circle and takes the next turn at selecting a ball and bouncing it behind another child. A child who fails to guess the correct ball misses that chance to be in the center of the circle.

Conversation: Does the size of the ball make a difference in the sound it makes?
Does what a ball is made of make a difference in the sound it makes?
Does it make a difference if the ball is hollow or solid?

70 • SHEPHERD AND SHEEP

Skill Development: 1. Auditory discrimination
2. Auditory association

Materials: 3 key chains with keys, 3 balls, 3 pairs of scissors, 3 small bags of rocks

Procedure: Construct a fenced off area for a sheep pen. Select three children to be shepherds. Give each shepherd one of each of the objects listed above. The other children are sheep that don't want to be in the pen. The shepherds try to get the sheep in the pen by walking up to one and asking it to turn its back. Then the shepherd drops one of the items on the floor behind the sheep. A sheep that can't call out the name of the dropped item must go into the pen. A sheep that correctly identifies the dropped item continues to be free. (Sometimes a more difficult assortment of items is necessary.)

Conversation: Do you think you hear the same from the back as you do from the front?

71 • MAY I?

Skill Development: 1. Following directions
2. Auditory memory

Materials: None

Procedure: Explain the following rules of the game. The children stand in a line at the back of the room. Call on each child and give one of the following directions:

Take _____ (number) giant steps.
Take _____ baby steps.
Take _____ hops.

Each child, after receiving the command, responds, "May I?" You reply, "Yes, you may" or "No, you may not." A child who forgets to ask "May I?" loses a turn. A child who moves after hearing "No, you may not" also loses a turn. The first child to make it to the front of the room is the winner. When the children know the commands, they may take turns giving them.

Conversation: By listening very carefully we can follow directions.

72 • 'TIS THE SEASON

Skill Development: 1. Auditory association
2. Critical listening

Materials: None

Procedure: With the children sitting on the floor, one child is selected as *It*. The other children close their eyes and the child who is *It* makes a statement about doing something seasonal. The first child who correctly guesses the activity and the season becomes *It*.

Examples:
I'm putting on my bathing suit.
(Going swimming in summer)

I've got to put my gloves on to make this ball.
(Making a snowball in winter)

Conversation: Are certain sounds associated with a season?
(Bee with spring)
If we couldn't see but only listened, could we identify the season? How?

73 • HULLY GULLY

Skill Development: 1. Auditory discrimination
2. Critical listening

Materials: A bag of glass marbles

Procedure: Introduce the children to the game of Hully Gully. Child 1 takes one to five marbles without letting anyone see how many. It is usually best to begin with three marbles. Child 1 then asks Child 2, "Do you want to play Hully Gully?" Child 2 says, "Yes." Then Child 1 shakes the hand holding the marbles so the marbles bounce off each other and asks, "Hully Gully, how many?" Child 2 tries to guess the correct number of marbles based on listening to them bumping together. If the guess is right, Child 2 gets the bag of marbles and moves to the next child.

Conversation: What does *estimate* mean?
What value is there in being able to estimate?
Can you think of a time when this skill is
  important?

Skill Development: 1. Auditory memory
2. Purposeful listening
3. Auditory sequencing

Materials: None

Procedure: Tell the children that they are going to take a pretend trip. The trip will be for two days and they are to think of things they need to take. Let the children talk about the trip and discuss things they would like to take. After the discussion, ask one child to mention a necessary item. Then the next child mentions that item and adds a second item. The third child names the first two items before adding a third item. Continue the game until the children can no longer remember all the items. Some practice may be necessary before the children understand what to do.

Examples:
1st child: I'm going on a trip and taking *shoes.*

2nd child: I'm going on a trip and taking *shoes* and *socks.*

3rd child: I'm going on a trip and taking *shoes, socks,* and *candy.*

Conversation: How do you listen carefully?
How can you remember what others have said?

75 • DOG AND BONE

Skill Development: 1. Auditory discrimination
2. Reactions to sounds
3. Listening for enjoyment

Materials: A chair and a rolled up newspaper

Procedure: Select a child to be the dog. The dog is blindfolded and seated in the chair. A bone (rolled up newspaper) is placed under the chair. Each child takes a turn trying to crawl up to the dog in the chair and steal the bone without being heard. The child who is caught becomes the dog.

Conversation: What can you hear with careful listening?
What are some small sounds you hear every day?
If you close your eyes, what sounds can you hear?

Music and Movement

Skill Development: 1. Auditory discrimination
2. Purposeful listening

Materials: Record player and instrumental records

Procedure: Play the records for the children and identify specific musical instruments for them. After identifying the instruments several times, ask the children if they can name them.

Conversation: Different instruments make different sounds, yet all are necessary for the music.

77 • WHICH ONE IS IT?

Skill Development: Auditory discrimination

Materials: Rhythm band instruments such as a bell, sticks, a tambourine, triangles, and cymbals

Procedure: Later in the year after the children have become familiar with the sounds of different instruments, organize them in small groups. Each group takes a turn standing back-to the table with rhythm instruments. One member of the group is selected to be the "musician." At your signal, the musician sounds one of the instruments. The other children raise their hands when they know which instrument it is. Vary the activity by selecting two children to be the "musicians." At your signal, both musicians sound an instrument. Can the other children identify both instruments? If not, the musicians sound their instruments separately. Be sure everyone gets a turn both sounding an instrument and identifying the sound.

Conversation: What are the different sounds and how are they made?
Does the shape of the instrument have anything to do with the sound it produces?

78 • MAKING MARACAS

Skill Development: 1. Purposeful listening
2. Following directions
3. Creative listening

Materials: Bucket, glue, water, newspapers, wooden spoon, old light bulbs, and crayons

Procedure: Explain to the children that they are going to make maracas by the following method:

1. In the bucket, make a mixture of glue and water.

2. Tear strips of newspaper and push them into the mixture with the wooden spoon.

3. Remove the soaked strips of paper from the mixture and wrap them around the bulbs to cover completely. Let the bulbs dry.

4. At least five times, repeat wrapping the bulbs with more soaked newspaper strips and letting them dry.

5. When the bulbs are completely dry, decorate them with crayons.

6. Rap each maraca sharply against the edge of a table. The glass bulb inside will shatter. When the maraca is shaken it will rattle.

Conversation: What makes the rattle?
Why doesn't the glass fall out?
Would this make a good rhythm instrument?

79 • XYLOPHONE

Skill Development: 1. Auditory discrimination
2. Creative listening

Materials: Xylophone

Procedure: Introduce the children to the xylophone by playing a simple tune. After the children experiment with the instrument for a few days, tell them that they are going to play a game in which different sounds mean different things. When you play the lowest note on the xylophone, the children will sit down, and when you play the highest note, they will stand up. After practicing a few times, tell the children you will try to fool them, but they should sit or stand only when those two notes are played. Alternate notes and sometimes play the same note twice. A child who does the wrong thing is eliminated from the game.

Conversation: On the xylophone, why are different colors used for different sounds?
What, besides color, is different between the high and low notes on the xylophone?

80 • TING TONG

Skill Development: 1. Auditory discrimination
2. Purposeful listening
3. Critical listening
4. Sound sequencing

Materials: Four water glasses, water, and a metal spoon

Procedure: Pour different amounts of water into each glass. When the glasses are tapped with the spoon, they will produce different sounds. Put the glasses where the children can observe you tapping them. Ask the children to listen for differences in the sounds produced. Have them arrange the glasses from lowest note to highest note and then from highest note to lowest note. Encourage experimenting by allowing the children to change the amount of water in a glass and noting the resulting change in sound.

Conversation: How did we change the sound in a glass?
Why do you think the amount of liquid in the glass is responsible for the sound produced?

Skill Development: 1. Auditory discrimination
2. Creative listening
3. Critical listening

Materials: A cigar box or similar box for each child and assorted rubber bands

Procedure: Tell the children they are going to have the opportunity to make a musical instrument. Ask them to listen carefully while you tell them how. Select six rubber bands of different sizes and place the bands around the box from end to end. When you pluck the rubber bands, they will produce different sounds according to their differences in size. The children may want to arrange the rubber bands from the lowest note to the highest note.

Conversation: Different sized rubber bands vibrate at different rates. The vibration produces sound.

82 • SING US A SONG

Skill Development: 1. Auditory association
2. Verbal creativity

Materials: Paper, pencil, a record player and a record of simple tunes without words or a tape player and taped music

Procedure: Ask the children to help you make up some words for the tunes they are going to hear. Each child takes a turn listening to a tune and supplying words. It doesn't matter what words the child uses. Sometimes it is best to let the child think for a while after listening to the songs. Write the child's words down and help the child select a title. Hang the paper on the wall or bulletin board.

Conversation: Why do songs have titles?
Do some tunes have more than one set of words?

83 • BEATING A RHYTHM

Skill Development: 1. Auditory discrimination
2. Auditory memory

Materials: Two sticks or a drum and drum sticks (optional)

Procedure: Explain that you are going to beat out (or clap) a rhythm. Ask the children to listen and repeat the rhythm by clapping. After practicing with one rhythm, ask different children to stand before the class and produce the rhythm for the other children to repeat. Then go on to the next rhythm.

Examples:
Two slow beats and two fast beats.
Two slow beats and three fast beats.
Three fast beats and two slow beats.

Conversation: Rhythm can be fast or slow.
Sounds can be loud or soft.
Counting the beats can make ryhthms easier to repeat.

84 • OLD MR. BOA CONSTRICTOR

Skill Development:
1. Auditory perception
2. Listening for information
3. Following directions

Materials:
The boa constrictor song (words are given below)

Procedure:
The children may sing with you or with a record or tape. Have the children act out the song by touching their body parts as they are mentioned in the song.

I'm being swallowed by a boa constrictor
A boa constrictor, a boa constrictor.
I'm being swallowed by a boa constrictor
And I don't like it one bit.

What do you know, he's swallowed my toe!
Oh gee, he's swallowed my knee!
Oh my, he's up to my thigh!
Oh fiddle, he's reached my middle!
Oh heck, he's up to my neck!
Oh dread, he's up to my . . . blaaahhhhhh!

Conversation:
Do you know the parts of the body?
Have you ever seen a snake?
What do snakes eat?
What do other animals eat?
How do you feel when you hear this song?

85 • DANCE TO DIRECTIONS

Skill Development: 1. Following directions
2. Auditory discrimination
3. Auditory appreciation

Materials: Record of "The Hokey Pokey"

Procedure: Play the record and instruct the children to follow the directions as they hear them.

Conversation: Can you listen to the words when music is playing and people are moving?
Can you follow the directions when everyone around you is moving?

86 • FREE MOVEMENT

Skill Development: Creative listening

Materials: Record player and records of fast and slow music

Procedure: Have the children listen to a music selection. Then play the music again and ask them to move freely while they listen. Encourage them to follow the music's moods and changes.

Conversation: How does the music make you feel?

What does it make you think of?

Nature and
Animals

87 • NAME THE ANIMAL

Skill Development: 1. Auditory discrimination
2. Auditory memory

Materials: A blindfold

Procedure: One child is blindfolded while the other children scatter around the room. One child at a time makes the sound of a familiar animal and the blindfolded child tries to identify the animal. After three animals have been successfully identified, another child is blindfolded. Other categories such as cartoon characters, vehicles, and street noises may be substituted for animals.

Conversation: What are some of the sounds different animals make?
Why do they make the sounds? Are they talking?

88 • SOUND GARDEN

Skill Development: 1. Purposeful listening
2. Auditory discrimination

Materials: Pencil-size sticks, string, markers, small strips of tagboard, plastic tape, rocks, and objects that will make noise when raindrops fall on them such as a tin pan, paper, cardboard, and a glass jar

Procedure: Explain that the children are going to make a sound garden for the next time it rains. Using the sticks and string, section off a five-foot-square garden outside the classroom windows. Use the markers, tagboard, and tape to label the objects. Weight the labels with rocks so they won't blow away. The next time it rains, open the windows and let the children listen to the differences in sound as the rain falls on different items.

Conversation: What are some sounds that different objects make when rain hits them?
Have you ever listened to the rain on the roof at night? Why does it sound different from rain falling on other things?

Skill Development: 1. Auditory discrimination
2. Critical listening
3. Listening for information
4. Auditory memory

Materials: Hose, tape recorder, blank recording tapes, heavy-duty extension cord, and sprinkler

Procedure: Warm or hot weather is the best time for this activity. Put a sprinkler outside but close to the classroom windows. Put a tape recorder, set to record, just outside the water area. Turn on the recorder. Birds will gather near the sprinkler to cool off, hunt for worms, and gather nest materials. Have the children stand quietly at the windows so they can see and hear the birds. Identify the birds and associate them with their bird calls. Later, bring in the tape recorder, play the tape, and ask the children to identify the birds by listening to the sounds they make.

Conversation: Why are birds attracted to water?
Why do different birds sound different?
Do we have the same birds all year?

Skill Development: 1. Auditory discrimination
2. Auditory memory
3. Creative listening

Materials: A book about zoo animals, heavy paper, crayons

Procedure: Read to the children about zoo animals. Review the reading selection, adding the sounds particular animals make. Ask different children to help make the animal sounds. Distribute the paper and crayons and ask each child to draw one zoo animal. After the children have finished drawing, ask them to take turns showing their pictures to the class and making the sounds the animals make.

Conversation: Do all animals make sounds?
How are the sounds alike and different?
Do some animals make loud sounds?
Do some animals make soft sounds?

91 • WHAT EATS WORMS?

Skill Development: 1. Listening for information
2. Critical listening
3. Relating information heard and factual knowledge

Materials: Pictures of animals such as a dog, pig, fish, and snake

Procedure: Stand the pictures in front of the seated children. Explain that you are going to talk about one of the animals and they are to identify that animal.

Example:
This animal swims in the water and likes to eat worms.

Conversation: How do different kind of animals behave differently?
What are some funny ways that animals behave?

Snack Time

92 • POPPING SOUNDS

Skill Development: 1. Auditory perception
2. Auditory association

Materials: Newspapers, popcorn popper, popcorn, (cooking oil, if needed)

Procedure: Spread newspapers over several square feet. Place the popcorn popper in the center of the newspapers. Seat the children in a semicircle facing the popper. Talk to the children about popping corn. Explain that you want them to count the number of pops they hear while the corn is popping. Also, ask them to observe how far popcorn travels when it is popped without a lid. Pop the corn as directed in the popper directions but without using a lid. When the popping stops, ask the children how many pops they heard and how far the corn traveled.

Conversation: Why does popcorn pop?
What can you do with popcorn other than eat it? What can you make? (Necklace, bracelet, collage, bird feeder, garlands, Christmas decorations)

93 • POPCORN BALLS

Skill Development: 1. Purposeful listening
2. Following directions

Materials: Corn popper, popcorn, molasses, bowls, half-cup measures, and waxed paper

Procedure: Tell the children how popcorn balls are made. Then announce that they are going to make some. Follow the directions for making popcorn. When the corn has finished popping, measure it into small bowls—1/2 cup to a bowl. Ask the children to wash their hands. Give a bowl of popcorn to each child. Measure the molasses by half-cups and instruct the children to pour it over their popcorn. Then they mix the popcorn and molasses with their hands, shape the mixture into balls and place the balls on waxed paper to harden.

Conversation: What causes corn to pop?
What is molasses made from?
What are some other things you can make or do with popcorn?

94 • SHARE THE COOKIE

Skill Development: 1. Critical listening
2. Purposeful listening
3. Creative listening

Materials: A package of cookies

Procedure: Pass out the cookies in a seemingly random way but giving only half the children a cookie. Explain that you have enough for only half the children. Ask how the problem could be solved. Accept all answers but look for the suggestion that a cookie can be broken in half and shared with someone. Stress that the whole cookie will make two pieces of cookie.

Conversation: A whole can be divided into parts and parts combine to make a whole.
Could the cookies have been shared with a larger group? How?

95 • FIRE DRILL OR SNACK TIME?

Skill Development: 1. Auditory association
2. Auditory discrimination
3. Purposeful listening

Materials: A bell and a bag of snacks

Procedure: Use this activity on a day that you have been alerted for a fire drill. Before the drill, show the children your bell and tell them that when you ring the bell you are going to pass out snacks. Later in the morning, ring the bell and pass out the snacks. Later in the day, the children will hear the bells for the fire drill. Ask them if that is the bell to signal snacks.

Conversation: Certain sounds have specific meanings. Can you match the right meaning to the sound? How did you know what to do when you heard each bell?

Let's Have a Discussion

Skill Development: 1. Critical listening
  2. Listening for information

Materials: Chalkboard and chalk or experience chart and marker, and strips and squares of posterboard

Procedure: Discuss listening with the children and why it is important. Discuss things that help a person listen and things that make it hard to listen. After the discussion, list rules for listening in the classroom. Ask the children to make suggestions and write them on the chalkboard or experience chart. With the children's help, select a few to be written on the posterboard and displayed on the wall.

Conversation: Why are rules necessary?
How will the rules we have written down make it easier to listen in the classroom?

97 • WHAT DID WE TALK ABOUT?

Skill Development: 1. Purposeful listening
2. Critical listening
3. Auditory memory

Materials: None

Procedure: Set aside a time every day for language development, including listening skills. As reinforcement, ask the children to remember from day to day what was discussed in the previous lesson. Call on a different child each day to summarize the language/listening lesson.

Conversation: Why is it important to remember what has been talked about in the past?
How are listening and speaking related.

Skill Development: 1. Purposeful listening
2. Auditory perception
3. Listening for problem solving
4. Listening for information

Materials: Chalkboard and chalk or experience chart and markers

Procedure: From time to time, someone such as a policeman or fireman will be a visiting speaker in the classroom. Use these occasions to improve listening skills. When you know a visitor will be coming the next day, discuss with the children what they think the visitor will talk about. Write the children's suggestions on the chalkboard or experience chart. After the visitor leaves, talk about what was discussed. Compare the visitor's topic with what the children suggested might be talked about.

Conversation: Why did the visitor talk to you?
What was most important point the visitor made?

Skills Index

The numbers following each skill category refer to the activity numbers.

Another program to develop listening skills . . .

CLAS K-2
Classroom Listening and Speaking (1985)
by Lynn Plourde, M.A., CCC-SLP

Have your whole year planned with this program. You'll have three year-long calendars—one each for kindergarten, first, and second grades—offering regular practice for speaking and listening skills. More than 200 activities promote learning in 12 target areas including Giving and Following Directions, Grammar, Rhyming and Reasoning. Each activity comes with a stated objective, materials list, time needed and suggested procedure.

Catalog No. 7327-Y $55

ALL ABOUT ME
Activities for Learning Language (1986)
by Constance F. McCarthy and Ann D. Sheehy

Help younger children develop pragmatic language skills and improve self-image with this collection of reproducible activities. These worksheets provide children with opportunities to learn and use basic language skills in developing self-awareness. You'll have worksheets for these topics—colors, shapes, concepts, senses, feelings, self-expression, body parts, clothing, and sequencing.

Catalog No. 7290-Y $19.95

Merle B. Karnes' EARLY CHILDHOOD RESOURCE BOOK (1985)
by Merle B. Karnes, Ed.D.

Here are 187 activities to enhance your preschool program . . . and strengthen language development. With this resource book, you can fill in your curriculum as you want. Tie these activities to your lessons or use them as lessons themselves.

Catalog No. 7275-Y $14.95

Communication Skill Builders ®

3830 E. Bellevue/P.O. Box 42050
Tucson, Arizona 85733
(602) 323-7500